# THE HEALTHY RELATIONSHIP
## @work

*Learn how to build great work relationships improving your <u>active listening</u>, <u>body language</u>, and <u>empathy</u> skills*

© **Copyright 2019 - All rights reserved.**

The content contained within this book may not be reproduced, duplicated or transmitted without direct written permission from the author or the publisher.

Legal Notice:

This book is copyright protected. It is only for personal use. You cannot amend, distribute, sell, use, quote or paraphrase any part, or the content within this book, without the consent of the author or publisher.

Disclaimer Notice:

Please note the information contained within this document is for educational and entertainment purposes only. All effort has been executed to present accurate, up to date, reliable, complete information. No warranties of any kind are declared or implied. Readers acknowledge that the author is not engaging in the rendering of legal, financial, medical or professional advice.

By reading this document, the reader agrees that under no circumstances is the author responsible for any losses, direct or indirect, that are incurred as a result of the use of information contained within this document, including, but not limited to, errors, omissions, or inaccuracies.

# Table of Contents

*Introduction* ............................................................. 1
   **The Importance of Social Skills in the workplace** ... 1
   **Social Skills to improve: short inventory** ............... 4
      Empathy ............................................................... 4
      Cooperation ......................................................... 5
      Verbal and Written Communication ................... 5
      Listening .............................................................. 5
      Nonverbal Communication ................................. 6
      Relationship management ................................. 6
      Conflict resolution .............................................. 6
      Respect for others ............................................... 7

*Chapter 1: How to Improve Your Social Skills* .......... 8
   **Essential Social Skills** ............................................. 9
      Disagree in an agreeable manner ..................... 10
      Do not assume things ....................................... 10
      Smile .................................................................. 11
      Maintain eye contact while talking .................. 11
      Be upbeat ........................................................... 12
      Be cognizant of your body language ................ 12
      Get involved ...................................................... 12
      Offer praise ........................................................ 13
      Have good intentions ....................................... 14

Be helpful ........................................................ 14
Take care of your health .................................. 14
Attitude counts................................................. 14
Be your best...................................................... 15

## Effective Communication Skills for the Workplace ..................................................................16

Show interest ................................................... 16
Use suitable nonverbal cues ........................... 17
Speak clearly .................................................... 17
Use a tone that is acceptable........................... 17
Develop appropriate listening skills .............. 18
Socialize in a new environment...................... 18
Be assertive but not aggressive ...................... 18
Select the right channels of communication ... 19
Be flexible and cooperate................................ 19
Do not be defensive and accept criticism ......20
Do something that you find challenging ......20
Show respect to others.................................... 21
Have patience................................................... 21
Say no to distractions...................................... 21
Show empathy..................................................22
Be confident ....................................................22
Be a skillful learner .........................................22
Learn to engage in small talk..........................23

*Chapter 2: Next step, how to properly use Body Language* .................................................................. 24
    Role of NonVerbal Cues in Communication .................... 25
**Understanding Concepts of Body Language:** ........ 26
**Use Gestures for Better Communication** .............. 30
    Hand gestures ................................................................ 30
    Move around .................................................................. 31
    Spot emblems ................................................................ 31
    Good posture ................................................................. 32
    Mirror the other person ................................................ 32
    Use gestures to emphasize a point ............................... 33
    Avoid using gestures that express insecurity or nervousness ................................................................... 33
**Decipher Facial Expressions** ................................. 34
    Visual dominance .......................................................... 34
    Eye contact can convey different messages .................. 34
    Emotions are conveyed through facial expressions ........ 35
    Improve Your NonVerbal Communication ..................... 36
    Read the Nonverbal Cues .............................................. 38
*Chapter 3: Time to practice. How to Have a Good Conversation* ......................................................... 41
**Steps for Having a Remarkable Conversation** ...... 41
**Conversation Starters** .......................................... 48
**Ways to Make Your Conversation Interesting** ..... 50
    Ask something personal in connection with the topic .... 50
    Bowing out in a group ................................................... 53

## Chapter 4: The downside, How to Improve Your Listening Skills .................................................. 55

### Listen Actively .................................................. 55

Face the person who is speaking and keep eye contact .. 56

Be attentive and relaxed ................................................. 57

Do not be judgmental ..................................................... 58

Create a picture in your mind ......................................... 58

Do not interrupt or impose solutions ............................. 59

Ask questions when there is a pause ............................. 60

Do not ask questions and distract the person from the topic ................................................................................. 60

Express empathy ............................................................. 61

Give regular feedback .................................................... 61

Note the nonverbal cues ................................................. 62

### The Five-Step Method for an effective Listening .. 62

Listen to audio without reading .................................... 63

Repeat .............................................................................. 64

Read ................................................................................. 64

Use both audio and text ................................................. 65

Listen to the audio once again ....................................... 65

## Chapter 5: They love you because you are empathetic .................................................................................. 66

### Best Ways to Express Empathy .......................... 67

Listen ............................................................................... 67

Open up ........................................................................... 67

Show physical affection ................................................. 68

Notice everything that is going on around you ............... 69

  Avoid judging others ....................................................... 70

  Offer to help the other person ........................................ 71

**The Responses to be Avoided** ............................... 72

  Do not dodge .................................................................... 72

  Look for the silver lining ................................................ 72

  Try to minimize things .................................................... 73

  Give advice ........................................................................ 73

  Tell stories ........................................................................ 73

  Talk about a worse case .................................................. 74

  Overreact .......................................................................... 74

*Tips to Develop Empathy* ........................................ *75*

  Take interest in people ................................................... 75

  Work as a volunteer ........................................................ 76

  Overcome your prejudices .............................................. 76

  Imagination ...................................................................... 77

  Experiential empathy ...................................................... 77

  Give importance to each one ......................................... 78

  Meditation ........................................................................ 78

  Practicing Empathy in the Workplace .......................... 79

  Do not use assumptions .................................................. 81

*Chapter 6: Outside of work. How to Meet People and Make New Friends* ................................................. *82*

**Opportunities for Meeting New People** ............. 82

  Take part in sports .......................................................... 82

| | |
|---|---|
| Book clubs | 83 |
| Writing groups | 83 |
| Meetup | 84 |
| Talk to your neighbors | 84 |
| Converse with people around you | 85 |
| Use community tables | 86 |
| Reach out to people through social media | 86 |
| Host a party | 87 |
| Go for a walk with your dog | 88 |
| Business associations | 88 |
| Go to the gym | 89 |
| Ask someone to introduce you to friends | 89 |
| Join a speaking club | 90 |
| Attend cultural events | 90 |
| Brew tours | 91 |
| Attend seminars | 91 |
| Go to a music club | 91 |
| Dance classes | 91 |
| Visit a museum | 92 |
| Art classes | 92 |
| Join a nonprofit organization | 93 |
| Coffee house | 93 |
| Go to a bar | 93 |
| Make the best use of invitations | 94 |
| Visit a farmers' market | 94 |

    Don't skip your class reunion............................................ 94
**Smart Ways of Making Friends............................ 95**
**Tips for Making Friends ........................................96**
**Top Friend Making Hacks for Shy People .......... 100**
    Approaching a shy person.............................................. 102
*Conclusion ........................................................104*
**Ways to enhance social skills ............................ 107**

# Introduction

Social skills are behaviors and other means of communication that are necessary to form and maintain relationships. This includes all relationships we have in life, whether it's with our partner, our children, our peers, our coworkers, or the mail delivery person. How we interact with others is the foundation of social skills.

We learn these skills as children from our parents, teachers and other adults we come in contact with on a regular basis. As we grow, our social skills become further developed, and for some, it isn't until the teen years that such things as shyness, anxiety and isolation are conquered.

This book will provide you with everything you need to improve your social skills.

## The Importance of Social Skills in the workplace

Social skills are also called 'soft' or 'interpersonal' skills. They play an important role in building personal as well as professional relationships. Gaining a proper understanding of social skills and improving them can help you in gaining success in any sphere of life.

Social skills are important for interactions in our everyday lives. Whether it's to make friends, initiate conversations, deal with bullies or unreasonable people, and practice good sportsmanship, social skills are paramount for effective communication.

Social skills have been linked to job success and overall well-being.

Each of us has our own personality, which determines our social skills. From childhood, we learn specific behaviors by picking up cues from those around us. This helps us to develop into who we are.

A shy, withdrawn person will have difficulty being social. Conversely, an outgoing person will small talk with strangers in line at the grocery store or while in a doctor's office waiting room. They are generally friendly, good natured, and nonjudgmental of others.

A shy, introverted person will not seek external stimulation from those around them. They will keep to themselves and often have difficulty communicating effectively.

No matter what type of success we are looking for, social skills are a critical component to thrive as an adult.

Scholars identify four markers for social skills and define them as:

- **Survival skills:** This includes listening, ignoring, and following directions.

- **Interpersonal skills:** This includes sharing, joining in a conversation, and take turns talking.

- **Problem-solving skills:** These skills include asking for help, deciding what to do, taking appropriate action, and recognizing when to apologize.

- **Conflict resolution skills:** These skills include handling teasing and bullying, being a good sport, and dealing with losing.

To have good social skills, we need to have good communication skills. Communication skills are more than verbal interactions. That means knowing nonverbal cues such as making eye contact, nodding, and keeping an open body posture.

Good communication skills also means learning how and when to say no. This can be one of the most difficult skills for many because we want to do for others, even if the request is unreasonable. Learning to say no without guilt and without offering excuses or reasons isn't an easy thing to do, but it is necessary.

We are social beings, so other people affect us and we can influence other using the tools we've at our disposal. We just need to identify and enhance them.

## Social Skills to improve: short inventory

Demonstrating good social skills in the workplace shows a willingness to get along with coworkers and to excel at your position; hence, leading to possible promotions and certainly better working relationships. The following are the traits needed for the work environment.

*Empathy*

Empathy is one of the most important skills. That is why I consider appropriate to dedicate a special section in that book to treat the subject (Chapter 5). In short, to introduce and simplify, when we interact with others, it's important to understand how the person feels. You might have a coworker who isn't working up to par or a client who has a problem. In both situations, you need to be a good listener, not jump to conclusions, and use your empath skills to help them. When they see you are genuinely concerned, they will feel comfortable speaking with you about whatever is on their minds.

*Cooperation*

Cooperation is essential if you work in a team environment or supervise employees. Remember that you are all working toward a common goal, and the way to reach that goal is by cooperating with those you work with. Getting along with all of your colleagues will guarantee that things will go smoothly if someday you are assigned to work with a colleague you don't normally work with.

*Verbal and Written Communication*

Verbal communication is the ability to express yourself by speaking clearly so that others can understand you. You want to express yourself by using appropriate (and correct) grammar and punctuation in both verbal and written communication. It is especially important to express yourself clearly and concisely when sending written communication as it can be easily misinterpreted.

*Listening*

Listening skills are paramount to communication. There is nothing worse than speaking to someone who isn't paying attention to what you're saying. You need to listen to your coworkers, supervisors and clients so that you know their needs. The last thing you want to do is to ask your boss to repeat an instruction because your mind was elsewhere. Just as you expect others to listen to you, you need to be listening to them. It's a sign of respect and genuine interest.

*Nonverbal Communication*

Your body language can tell the person you're conversing with quite a bit. Body language is nonverbal communication that we send or receive by using eye contact and facial expressions.

*Relationship management*

This refers to the knack of building key connections and maintaining relationships. It is especially useful for people who play certain roles in the workplace. For instance, a customer service agent is responsible for managing the relationship between his company and its clients. Executives of various companies manage the relationships with investors or stakeholders.

*Conflict resolution*

There can be dissatisfaction and disagreements in any workplace. Conflict resolution refers to a person's capacity to find the root of a problem and arrive at a suitable solution. It's an important trait to have, especially for those who work in large companies where there tends to be more personality clashes.

*Respect for others*

Allowing the other person to speak without interruptions is an essential communication skill whether you are in a one-to-one conversation or in a group setting. It is a way of showing respect to the speaker. This is easy to do in a face-to-face conversation because you are looking at the person and you know when they are speaking and when they are finished. On the phone, it can be different because there can be a delay. That delay can result in interruptions as it can appear the other person has stopped speaking when they really haven't. Allow a pause to be certain the person has finished before beginning to talk when on the phone.

Now that you know the importance of social skills, let's look at how you can improve.

# Chapter 1: How to Improve Your Social Skills

As we said, humans are social beings. Each individual feels the need to be loved and accepted in society. Social interaction plays a significant role in our lives.

While researchers have proven that extroverts are generally more successful in their endeavors and more social, it's not a bad thing to be an introvert.

Introverts are great observers and listeners. They will absorb everything around them, although they might not contribute to a conversation, even if they have something beneficial to offer. They are shy and often insecure. Fear of saying the wrong thing and coming off as foolish will keep an introvert from opening up in conversation. This can be an obstacle in the path to success for the introvert.

When a person is able to present his ideas accurately and connect with others, there are more chances of being successful and it becomes easier to achieve success.

# Essential Social Skills

Today, people spend their time mostly in the digital world instead of the real world. You have probably seen those types of people–they sit across from each other at a restaurant table and they are on their phones, never looking up, never conversing.

When it comes time to converse, they have limited words for the other as they are too wrapped up in whatever it is that's on their phone distracting them.

We see this more often with the younger generation, but the older generation is not immune from this antisocial behavior.

The digital age has changed the way we communicate, and it's not always for the better. Sure, it saves time when we can message a coworker instead of walking to their office. It saves time to be able to text the boss when they're out of town rather than to leave a message at the hotel where they are staying or having them paged when they're at a conference. Those were the good ole days before the advent of the cell phone. Often, emergencies had to wait, and employees were left unsure of what to do until the boss returned.

Sadly, the advent of cell phones led to the fracture of our social skills. This is why we sometimes need to relearn these skills to bring up back up to par. What we gained in social skills in our youth can fall into the abyss with technology.

Here is a list of skills that can help to increase your skills and be successful in the social sphere.

*Disagree in an agreeable manner*

The underlying basis of good communication is proper understanding. If someone says something that is not in line with your thinking, you need to be diplomatic about disagreeing.

You can begin by saying, "In all due respect…" This tells the person that you respect their opinion, but you are of a varying one. Then you can give your point of view. By letting the person you're speaking with know that you understand their opinion, you won't come off as confrontational or as a know-it-all.

You can also begin with a phrase such as, "I see your point, but…" A non-confrontational and non-disagreeable segue will put you on level ground.

*Do not assume things*

Assumptions can be dangerous. Never assume something. Always be sure before speaking. We have all heard of or been in situations when someone assumes something, and it's the wrong assumption. Conjecture can cause hurt feelings and much more. Assumptions aren't more than mere gossip, and gossip won't improve anyone's social status, and it's certainly not something you want to include in your skillset.

*Smile*

A smile can work wonders. It is easy to make friends and break the barriers between people by offering a pleasant smile. It can make others feel happy and show them that you care for them.

*Maintain eye contact while talking*

When you are talking to someone, your eyes should be on them. This doesn't mean to stare at them. It's okay to look away from time to time; however, eye contact lets the other person know that you are genuinely interested in what they're saying. When you don't look at the speaker, they will assume you're distracted. You might be listening intently, but they will assume otherwise. This is why assumptions aren't a good thing.

This also brings us back to our conversation about the digital age. When someone is speaking to you, don't be looking at you phone, or worse, texting. You need to focus on the speaker, not on Facebook or texting your significant other. Not only is it rude, but it tells the other person that you're not interested in what they're saying.

*Be upbeat*

Keeping a conversation positive and upbeat will relax the person you're talking with, and the more relaxed, the more comfortable the conversation.

Surely, there's been a time when you've had a tense conversation, or there was an awkwardness that crept into it. When you remain upbeat, you can keep any awkwardness away.

*Be cognizant of your body language*

When you are speaking one-on-one or in a group, you want to be relaxed and hold yourself in a non-threatening way. By that, it means you don't want to appear disinterested or as if you're ready to dart at the first open opportunity.

Keep your hands away from your face, watch how you stand or sit, and be cognizant of the position of your legs and arms. Don't tilt your head so far to one side that you appear to be disinterested or bored.

*Get involved*

The best way to build healthy relationships is to be involved in extracurricular activities. This is especially good for those who are trying to develop better social skills but are shy or don't have many contacts. Getting involved in a hobby or sport, take classes, attend church functions, etc. There's an endless list of ways to meet others and to build on social relations.

*Offer praise*

You should make it a point to praise others. Always look for opportunities to appreciate the good work done by others. It helps to create an amicable environment, and everyone feels happy when their hard work and efforts are given due recognition.

You don't want to do it to patronize someone because that can be very transparent. You need to be sincere and don't ramble on as if you're trying to convince the person that you are sincere. A simple "Great work" or "You really knocked that one out of the ballpark" lets that person know you are genuine and appreciate their work.

You can offer compliments as well, again, as long as you're sincere. Don't tell a female coworker that you love her scarf if it's completely tacky with the rest of her outfit. Don't tell a male boss that his tie is awesome if it looks like it was stolen from a clown.

Praise and compliments go hand-in-hand with honesty. A pretentious compliment will not go unnoticed.

*Have good intentions*

Always have good intentions. No matter what the situation, make sure your intentions are well-placed. Everyone makes mistakes; however, as long as it's not done with ill intentions, others will realize it.

*Be helpful*

Strive to help others, even when you might not be in the mood. Of course, you don't want to force help. If someone doesn't want it, you simply tell them that you're available if they change their mind. At least you made the offer.

*Take care of your health*

Everyone likes energetic people. A person's energy level depends on their health. The better you feel, the more confidence you'll have. You want to maintain a healthy diet and sleep habits. We won't elaborate on this as there's many books on the market that will guide you to better health if that's what you need.

*Attitude counts*

Have you ever spent a day with Debbie or Donnie Downer? It's certainly no fun to be around someone who always sees the glass as half-full, or worse, empty. They have a tendency to bring down others with their negative attitude.

You definitely don't want to be that person. You want to have a positive attitude, especially around your coworkers. A negative attitude can cost you a promotion. When looking at employees to advance, an employer will look for the employee with the most positivity. Those with a positive attitude are more successful and get father ahead in life.

You want to live your life so that when you leave this earth, people are sad and not celebrating that you're gone and took your miserable attitude with you. It's a sad fact. No one wants to be remembered for being cranky and uncooperative.

*Be your best*

Be what you are because that is the reason why people are fond of you. There is no need to pretend. You should display your best traits and be positive, flexible, and happy. People will love to associate with you and enjoy your friendship.

The same thing is applicable to the place where you work. There is no need to alter your personality to keep up with the company culture. You just have to be mindful of certain things and adjust to various social situations.

# Effective Communication Skills for the Workplace

Communication is the center of any business. To be effective, everyone needs to have excellent communication skills from the CEO to the custodian.

Even if you are highly qualified and also know how to do your work very well, if you lack social skills it may be tough for you to fit in with your coworkers.

If you have a job that requires you to interact with your colleagues and clients every day, it is important to learn and brush up the social skills that are required. You may be wondering how you can beat social phobia or enhance interpersonal skills. The following tips can be handy for becoming more assertive and confident in your workplace.

*Show interest*

This is a simple rule that many people overlook. You need to show a genuine interest in those you speak with. Don't be self-absorbed and talk only of yourself. This will quickly turn off those around you, and you could become known as a self-centered person.

If you take more interest in others and listen to what they are saying, you can build a good relationship with your colleagues.

*Use suitable nonverbal cues*

Good conversation does not only depend on what is said; it is also influenced by the way words are said. Nonverbal cues offer a lot of information when you are communicating with someone, and you can convey many things, even without saying a word.

You may offer some great information, but if you deliver it in an unenthusiastic manner, others may also not show any enthusiasm about it. You should not appear to be shy or closed off. Your stance should be confident. You should stand erect, sit with your back straight, and keep your hands on your sides instead of crossing them.

*Speak clearly*

It is important to speak clearly when conversing with your coworkers. If you feel that your speech is not clear, practice talking at a slower pace. Avoid mumbling as it may seem as if you are not interested in the particular discussion.

*Use a tone that is acceptable*

Do not speak very loudly and disturb others who are working in the same office. At the same time, you should be careful not to speak so softly that others have to struggle to hear you. If you are unsure about the tone that is permissible, observe your colleagues. Note the tone and pitch that they use to communicate and do the same.

*Develop appropriate listening skills*

There is a difference between hearing someone and listening actively. For example, you may have experienced that at times when you talk to your coworkers their attention becomes diverted. This may seem quite rude. But sometimes you also do the same thing without realizing it. Therefore, next time when someone talks to you make it a point to listen attentively.

*Socialize in a new environment*

If you practice socializing in new social settings that are different from the usual ones, it can help you to overcome the anxiety you have about socializing and boost your confidence. Once you become habituated to moving about in different social environments, it will be easier for you to interact with people in your workplace. It may be a good idea to join a dancing class or take up any hobby that interests you. This will give you a chance to mingle with new people.

*Be assertive but not aggressive*

There is a difference between these two types of behaviors. It is good to assert yourself and put forth your opinions, but you should not be so passionate about it that you go beyond a certain limit when it may seem that you are trying to refute what the other person is saying or trying to prove that they are wrong. If you are on the verge of being offensive, you are entering the aggressive mode.

When the conversation is about to become offensive, you should just steer it away from that topic and avoid an unwanted heated discussion.

*Select the right channels of communication*

There are varied ways of communicating with people. Make sure that you choose the right one. For instance, you should never use social media or email for putting forth an argument or conflict. Email does not carry any emotions, and it is difficult to share feelings and empathy through your computer. It is better to talk personally with someone than on the phone. The drawback about written conversation is that even if you use a comma in the wrong place, the meaning can change drastically.

*Be flexible and cooperate*

It is essential to be flexible and cooperate with others. You should not think that your method of doing things is the only right way. There may be plenty of other methods that other people use that might be equally suitable. You must remember to achieve anything you need the help of other people. You should be willing to share your ideas and also accept the suggestions given by others if they are right.

*Do not be defensive and accept criticism*

Nobody is perfect, and anyone can make mistakes. You should understand that constructive criticism in the workplace plays an important role in progress, so you should accept it without any bad feelings.

If someone opposes your view or criticizes your work, do not become defensive. Listen in a composed manner, and do not react immediately. If it is done by someone who has more experience than you, accept it. Although it is not very easy to take criticism, it is a social skill to listen to what is being said in an open manner and be ready to accept it.

*Do something that you find challenging*

Do the things that you are hesitant about. This will help you to become more sociable. For example, if public speaking is not your strong point, offer to make a presentation or hold a team meeting. It will help you to gain more knowledge as well as experience. You will learn how to deal with such situations.

*Show respect to others*

You may occupy a high position in your career, but do not forget to be respectful to others. You can give due regard to the feelings of others and show that you care for them as well as honor and admire them. Do not behave as if you possess higher knowledge and experience than the others and they are inferior to you. Being humble and mindful are good social skills that a person should possess.

Practicing good manners or saying "thank you" may make a lot of difference in the interactions with your colleagues. Besides this, you must also respect the personal space of others. Do not be invasive by disturbing them while they are at work or touching them.

*Have patience*

Patience is a great virtue. It is very useful for the workplace where you have to deal with many people. For example, you should allow the others to finish explaining everything before you jump to conclusions. This can help to avoid misunderstandings as well as confrontations.

*Say no to distractions*

There are so many things like social media, radio, TV, phones, and tablets that can distract us at work as well as make us separate ourselves from the people around us. To engage yourself sincerely in work and to focus on people who are working with you, it is necessary to avoid these distractions.

*Show empathy*

Develop the capacity to keep yourself in another person's situation and see things from their point of view. This will enable you to understand and appreciate the things put forth by others.

*Be confident*

If you have more confidence, you can interact with people better and be more sociable. Other people in the workplace may feel more at ease in approaching you and engaging in conversations with you. Whereas, if you are timid and shy, they may not come to you because they do not want you to feel awkward.

*Be a skillful learner*

Good entrepreneurs never stop learning. They are always on the lookout for ways things can be done more efficiently and effectively. You should always be ready to learn from others. If you are a good learner, you will be humble and imbibe lessons from the people around you. Your quest for knowledge will enable you to ask questions and get the solutions from experts who love to share their ideas with sincere seekers.

*Learn to engage in small talk*

It can go a long way in building relationships. Good salesmen have the art of engaging in small talk and making their clients feel special. Small talk portrays your personality effectively and helps you to connect with people beyond the business matters.

# Chapter 2: Next step, how to properly use Body Language

The ability to communicate properly is very important for success in any personal or professional relationship. Every time you interact with someone, you convey something verbally and also give a lot of information through the nonverbal cues. Your physical behavior, mannerisms, and expressions that are instinctively done make a great impact on the conversation.

When you are interacting with people, you continuously give and receive wordless signals. These can make others feel at ease, draw them toward you, and build trust. Otherwise, they can confuse, offend and undermine your effort to convey something. You do not stop sending these messages when you become silent. Even during that time you continue to communicate nonverbally.

Sometimes people say something but their body language conveys something else. For example a person may say 'yes' but shake their head as if to say 'no.' When a speaker sends mixed signals like this, the listener may feel that they are being dishonest. Since the nonverbal cues are natural and occur unconsciously, they demonstrate a person's true intentions and feelings. So when the listener has to choose whether to go by your verbal or nonverbal communication, he will pick the latter.

By understanding and using nonverbal communication in a better way, you can convey exactly what you mean, connect well with people and build more rewarding and stronger relationships.

*Role of NonVerbal Cues in Communication*

- **Compliment:** They compliment or add to what is said. For example, when a boss pats the back of an employee and praises him, the message can have a greater impact.

- **Substitute:** They can act as a substitute for the message that has to be conveyed verbally. For example, a person's facial expression can convey a much more vivid message compared to what is expressed through words.

- **Accent:** They can underline or accentuate the verbal message. For example, if a person pounds the table while speaking, it can make the message appear important.

- **Repeat:** They repeat and strengthen what is said verbally.

- **Contradict:** They can contradict what is being said and indicate that the person is not speaking the truth.

## Understanding Concepts of Body Language:

### Body language that conveys openness

- In this, a person has a relaxed posture but keeps their back straight. It shows that they are confident and comfortable.

- They keep their legs slightly apart. It demonstrates confidence. They lean in a little while talking to someone to show their interest. They do not lean away because that is a sign of hostility.

- They do not cross their arms. They keep their arms on their sides or keep them together on their lap, which shows that they are open to others.

- Their handshake is assertive and firm. They maintain eye contact. But they do not stare and are not intimidating.

- They speak in a tone that conveys confidence.

### Body language that conveys emotions

- If a person's face is flushed, and they clench their fists, it shows they are angry.

- If their face is pale and their mouth is dry so that they drink water or lick their lips, it shows that they are anxious or nervous. Also, their tone of speaking may vary and their muscles may be tense so they might clench their hands or arms. They might show other symptoms of nervousness such as trembling lips, gasping, holding breath, or fidgeting.

## Body language that shows a person is lying

- A liar may not keep eye contact. Their pupils may appear constricted.

- They might turn their body away.

- A change in complexion, such as redness of face or neck, perspiration, and vocal changes may indicate that a person is lying.

However, some signs like sweating and lack of eye contact can also be indications of fear or nervousness.

## Indications of disengagement

- When a person's head is tilted downward or their eyes are gazing elsewhere, it indicates disengagement.

- Fiddling, doodling, and slumping in a chair also show that an individual is disengaged.

## Blocking behavior

- If a person crosses their arms or sits behind the monitor of a computer while talking to someone, it exhibits a blocking behavior.

- While giving a speech or presentation, a person may prefer to have some sort of physical barrier between themselves and the audience, such as podiums, chairs, computers or a folder.

## Spacing

There are different ideas regarding the amount of physical space that should be given to another person in different cultures. Social distance can be divided into four categories. They are:

- **Intimate distance:** It is a distance of 1.5 feet from another person. If someone enters the intimate distance of another person, it may be unsettling for them if they have not asked for it. But it may be all right if they are already intimate with each other.

- **Personal distance:** It is between one to two feet. At this distance, the individuals are quite close; they can shake hands with each other and see their partner's gestures and expressions.

- **Social distance:** It is between two and four feet. This distance is normally maintained in impersonal situations or during business transactions. In this distance, a person has to speak loudly and eye contact is given importance.

- **Public distance:** It is between four to six feet. Teachers and those who have to talk to groups usually maintain this distance. In this distance, nonverbal cues are very important but they are often exaggerated. Head movements and hand gestures have a greater significance compared to facial expressions because the latter may not be perceived easily.

**Identify your patterns**

Think about what you do with your body during the different interactions that you have with various people. You can use a mirror to observe your posture and facial expressions when you are happy, nervous, or angry. In this way, you can identify your patterns of body language.

Assess whether the body language that you use synchronizes with the message you are trying to convey. Your nonverbal cues are effective if they communicate the message that you wish to communicate.

See if there is a disparity, and your posture shows that you lack confidence but your words exhibit confidence.

If your body language matches your words, you will communicate better and also be more charismatic.

## Use Gestures for Better Communication

*Hand gestures*

Experts say that great speakers make use of hand gestures in the course of presentations and conversations. According to them, these gestures enhance the confidence of the listeners in the particular speaker.

Complex gestures in which both the hands are used above the level of a person's waist are connected to complex thinking.

Politicians who are considered to be charismatic and are effective speakers usually use a lot of hand gestures. For example, Tony Blair, Barack Obama, and Colin Powell are all known to use hand gestures for more effective communication.

However, while using hand gestures you should remember that they should match your intentions and words. Otherwise, they may not convey the right message.

*Move around*

Great speakers not only move their hands, they also move around in the place. They do not keep themselves distant from people, instead they point to slides and are animated.

If a person keeps their hands in their pockets while speaking, it gives an impression that they are closed off and insecure. It's best to keep your hands out of your pockets, and keep your palms upward. This will show that you can be believed and trusted.

*Spot emblems*

They refer to gestures that are word equivalents. They may be accepting or passive. You should keep in mind that an emblem can have a different meaning in another culture.

- Tension in a person's body or clenched fists indicate aggression. They show that a person is preparing to fight. Making sudden movements can also show aggression.

- Gentle and slow gestures are considered to be accepting gestures. Keeping the arms rounded and the palms sideway, which looks like the individual is offering a hug, is an example of such a gesture. It also includes the act of nodding when another person is speaking. It shows that you accept the ideas of the person, and also makes you appear to be an effective listener.

*Good posture*

When a person maintains a bad posture on important occasions, such as his job interview, they can present a bad impression and perform poorly in the interview. Bad posture is often associated with lack of confidence or engagement and boredom. The interviewer might even think that the person is unmotivated and lazy if they do not sit erect.

To maintain a good posture, you should keep your head up and see to it that your back is straight. You can lean forward when you are sitting and talking to show that you are interested in the conversation.

*Mirror the other person*

When a person positions themselves in the same manner as the person they're speaking with, it is referred to as mirroring. The idea behind this is that when a person copies their partner's actions, it makes them feel connected.

A person can mirror the other person's body language or tone. But this should be done subtly and not repeatedly or blatantly.

Mirroring is a very effective way of using body language for building a good rapport with another person.

*Use gestures to emphasize a point*

- Although it is not necessary to make use of a gesture for each word, it is very helpful if you have a number of gestures to convey your messages. You can utilize them to reinforce important concepts that are easily misinterpreted. If the listeners are not able to pick up one gesture, they may surely be acquainted with another one.

- Direct the gestures that are positive toward your listener. This helps you to indicate clearly that you want a positive outcome. You should direct the gestures that are negative away from the listener and yourself. This will help you to clearly show that you do not want any obstacle in conveying your message.

*Avoid using gestures that express insecurity or nervousness*

- Wandering eyes, picking the fluff on clothing with your hands, and sniffling constantly are some gestures that should be avoided.

- If a person constantly touches their face or is hunched over, they will not look approachable, at ease, or confident. Getting rid of nervous tics takes time. But once they are eliminated, a person's overall communication can improve to a great extent.

## Decipher Facial Expressions

*Visual dominance*

The ratio of visual dominance is determined on the basis of a person looks more at the eyes of the other person and who looks away more. When you are speaking with someone, make an effort to look the person in the eyes to show confidence.

- A person's ratio of visual dominance indicates where he stands in the hierarchy of social dominance compared to his partner with whom he is having a conversation. Those who look away almost all the time have low social dominance.

- Those who mostly look downward show helplessness. It appears as if they are trying to avoid conflict or criticism.

*Eye contact can convey different messages*

Actually you can learn plenty of things about an individual by observing the way they use their eyes.

- If they avoids eye contact or look downward most of the time, it indicates defensiveness.

- If an individual is making an effort to listen, they will maintain more eye contact.

- If they look away when he is speaking, it suggests that they are not yet in a position to stop talking and listen.

- Looking at another person can also indicate that the individual is attracted to them. When someone has an interest in another person, their eye contact is strong, and they lean forward toward their partner.

- According to the context, eye contact may be used for showing respect. For instance, during a presentation when there are many people in the room, you can divide the room into three sections. Address your comments to the people on one side, then to those on the opposite side, and finally to those in the middle section. For this you can pick one person in every section and address your comments to them. Those who are seated around these individuals will feel that you are interacting with them directly. This will improve your rating, and you will be an effective speaker.

*Emotions are conveyed through facial expressions*

You should observe the facial expressions of a person during a conversation. This will help you to know the emotions of the person.

- Facial expressions that offer feedback in the course of a conversation are referred to as regulators. For example, nodding your head or expressions that show boredom or interest. Regulators enable the other individual to evaluate the level of agreement or interest in what is being said.

- You can express empathy toward the other individual through affirmative movements, such as nodding and smiling. If these gestures are used when the other individual is speaking, they provide positive reinforcement to that person and show that you like whatever they are saying.

*Improve Your NonVerbal Communication*

This sort of communication takes place very rapidly and you have to concentrate fully on what you experience each and every moment. If you plan what should be said next, think about random things or check your phone, you will miss many of the nonverbal cues and fail to comprehend the subtle points that are being communicated.

Besides remaining fully present during the conversation, you need to learn how to handle stress and develop emotional awareness to improve your nonverbal communication.

**Manage stress**

Stress undermines your capacity to communicate. If you are stressed you may misread the cues that you receive from other people and send confusing nonverbal signals to others. Your behavior patterns may be inappropriate. Emotions are usually contagious. So if you happen to be upset, you make those around you upset and turn a situation from bad to worse.

When you feel stressed, take a few moments to cool down before engaging in the conversation again. After regaining your emotional balance, you will be in a better position to handle things in a more positive way.

Employing your senses to see, smell, hear, touch, and taste is the surest and fastest way to make yourself calm and deal with stress at a particular time. Viewing your child's or pet's photo, smelling your favorite scent, squeezing a stress ball, or listening to music can also help to relax quickly and refocus. Each one can have a different sensory experience that works for them.

**Develop emotional awareness**

If you want to send the right signals, you must know about your emotions as well as the impact they have on you. You should also have the ability to identify other people's emotions and feelings conveyed by the cues that they send. To do this, you need to have emotional awareness.

If you are emotionally aware it will enable you to:

- Read others accurately, including the nonverbal messages they send and the emotions they experience.

- Gain the trust of people by sending unspoken messages that match your words.

- Show other people that you care for them and understand them by responding in an appropriate manner.

Many people are not able to connect with their strong emotions like fear, sadness, and anger because they have always been told that these feelings should be shut off. However, a person can numb or deny his feelings, but they cannot eliminate them. They continue to exist and affect a person's behavior.

If you become emotionally aware and connect even with the emotions that are unpleasant, you will have more control over the way you think or act. For this, you can practice mindfulness meditation or use some other technique that suits you.

*Read the Nonverbal Cues*

To gain a proper understanding of what the person is trying to convey, you should not only listen to his words but also observe and assess the nonverbal signs that accompany their speech.

While doing so it is necessary to:

- Observe inconsistencies between the message that is conveyed verbally and nonverbally.

- Look at all the nonverbal cues that you receive in a group from the tone of speaking, eye contact, gestures made by the person, to the position of their body. When they are put together, do they convey the same message as the words that are being said?

- Trust what your instincts tell you.

**Evaluate nonverbal signals**

- Facial expression: Is the person's face inexpressive and mask-like, or does it show that they are emotionally present and full of interest?

- Eye contact: Observe whether the person's eye contact is just right or overly intense.

- Tone: Does the tone of the individual's voice project confidence, interest, and warmth? Does it appear to be blocked and strained?

- Touch: See if there is some physical contact. Is it suitable for the situation? Is it comforting or discomforting?

- Posture: Is the individual's body immobile and stiff or is it relaxed? Are the shoulders raised and tense, or are they relaxed?

- Intensity: Do they appear to be disinterested and cool, or are they overly excited and melodramatic?

- Sounds: Can you hear any sounds that indicate the person is interested or concerned?

- Timing and pace: Does the conversation flow properly? Do the nonverbal responses appear too slowly or too quickly?

# Chapter 3: Time to practice. How to Have a Good Conversation

Everyone aspires to have an incredible, dazzling, and memorable conversation. For this, it is important to know how to start a great conversation, continue it in an interesting manner, and end it smoothly.

Ernest Agyemang Yeboah has said, "Sweet conversation is good for the heart and a good pill for forgetting bitter and wasteful thoughts; for a moment, it mutes so many bad thoughts and it keeps the heart calm" (Pills For Healthy Life).

## Steps for Having a Remarkable Conversation

### Purpose

You should have a clear goal. Just like you never drive to a new place without knowing the address, you should not engage in a directionless conversation. Indulging in an interaction without a suitable game plan can be compared to driving without being suitably equipped with a map.

If you wish to have a dazzling conversation and get dates and business connections from your meetings, you should identify your aim before going to events, parties, and meetings.

To be a good conversationalist, you must prepare, practice, and execute like a good athlete with the aim to win. Therefore, you should set your goals, know something about those you are going to meet, and do sufficient research to be well-prepared for the occasion.

While doing this, see if you can answer these questions regarding the event.

Who is the host of the event?

When is the event and what is the agenda?

What type of people will be there?

Why are you going there?

It is all right to have a simple reasons for going there, such as to get new customers or to enjoy time with others. This will enable you to have a purpose while talking with people. Everyone likes people with direction. Purpose is contagious; it gives confidence and enhances influence.

**The right approach**

Meet people with the right attitude. Approach them as a friend and not as a foe.

Maybe you think that people make their first impression only when they start talking. However, this is a wrong notion. The first impression is made even before that. When the other person sees you for the first time, they notice your confident and open body language.

You should give the right signals of being friendly. For instance, your hands should be visible and shoulders should be relaxed. You can smile and greet people.

**Use the technique of bookmarking**

You can use this technique to mark or emphasize certain parts of your dialogue that can help in creating deeper connections.

Bookmarks are actually verbal markers that make follow-up easy and give you a topic you can talk about later.

Types of bookmarks:

Future events: While speaking about conferences, if a person you like mentions that they are going to attend a conference in a few weeks and you are also going, you might say that you will be there too and it would be nice to have coffee together after the speeches. You can bookmark it in this way and follow up later.

Interesting incidents: When you are talking with a person and some funny or interesting thing takes place, you can bookmark it and use it later. For example, if you were chatting with someone in the park and you opened a packet of cookies to offer to the other person, and a dog jumped in the middle and sat between both of you, touching your hand with his paw, you might both be surprised by the dog's sudden appearance. Perhaps the dog stayed there and refused to move until he had finished all the cookies, then went away and returned with a ball. The dog put it in front of you and wagged its tail as if to say "Thanks for the treat." You can bookmark it and laugh about it whenever you are about to share some edibles in the future.

Some similarity: Sometimes you may come to know certain things that are similar for both of you. For instance, you may meet someone who has two elder brothers who are two and five years older than them, just like you. You can bookmark it and say that you are lucky to find someone who is in a similar family situation and can understand what it is like to be the youngest in the family and to live with two elder brothers.

Sharing things: When you are talking about articles, books, or videos and someone shows interest in them, you can bookmark it. For example you can say that you will send them the link for it so that they can have a look. This may prompt them to share some of their favorite stuff with you.

**Look for something exciting**

After you start talking, it is necessary to keep the dialogue interesting, so you should look for some conversation sparks.

This is what most of the charismatic people do. They ask questions, introduce topics, and put forth ideas that light up the conversation and kindle excitement.

So try to find the things that the person is excited about and talk about them instead of chit-chatting in a directionless manner and having awkward lulls during the interaction.

Usually, the topic that triggers dopamine makes a person feel excited. So it is a good idea to bring up a topic that enables a person to experience joy.

Some examples of sparking questions are:

- Do you have any plans for a big vacation in the next few months?
- Have you been working on something exciting recently?
- Have you seen any interesting movies recently?
- Are you pursuing some hobbies that you are passionate about?

**Nonverbal cues**

Raising the eyebrows is an enjoyable trick of nonverbal communication. Almost in all cultures, people raise their eyebrows when they come across something interesting. So if you notice this unspoken cue during a conversation, you should understand that the topic arouses the individual's curiosity, and he may be interested in discussing it.

For example, you may be engaged in a casual conversation about sports. When you mention the name of a certain famous player who studied in your school, the other person may raise their eyebrows. You can guess that he is a fan of that person and talk more about him and hold an interesting conversation.

## Tell enchanting stories

Stories make a conversation more captivating. People tend to grasp an idea and remember things more easily with the help of stories or anecdotes. But you should not monopolize the conversation and give a chance to the other person to tell his story as well.

## Mutual interaction

Do not hold a lopsided conversation. Even if you tell great stories or exhibit excellent body language, if you do not allow the other person to participate equally, they might avoid talking to you.

There should be reciprocity in a conversation. When a person shares something, they hope that the person they are speaking with will share a similar story. Likewise, when they ask a question, they hope to get a proper answer. So whether you are the speaker or the listener, make sure that there is equal give and take on both sides.

Another mistake to avoid when engaging in a conversation is trying to show that your experience is slightly more than the other person. Do not try to outdo someone. For example, if the other person says that they did not have a good day, you need not say that your day was worse. Or, if they say they have traveled to five countries, you do not need to say you have been to ten countries, even if you have. Give the other person a chance to revel in his own happiness.

**End smoothly**

Ending the dialogue on a suitable note and making a good last impression also has a lot of significance. You can use the bookmarks you have made earlier for ending your conversation. That means you can touch upon something interesting that you came across during the interaction. Use whatever subject applies to you at the time.

**Recollect and analyze**

It is quite possible that when you return home after a date or event, you may be very tired and wish to go straight to bed. However, it is advisable to recollect all that took place. You can do this while driving home, talking to your roommate or spouse, or writing a journal.

Try to answer these questions:

- What are the things that went well?
- What did you learn?
- Who is the person you should follow up with?

Recapitulation will help you to learn from your experience and polish your social skills.

## Conversation Starters

Sometimes, we find ourselves in situations where we aren't quite sure how to start a conversation.

You can use various starters to begin a conversation. You can ask a question or make a comment that can break the ice and start a dialogue with someone.

For example, you can say something about the wine or the venue.

These icebreakers serve as a building block in the formation of relationships, be they short or long term. When we come upon someone new, we can't start out by talking about your daughter's upcoming wedding or how much you enjoyed the latest Netflix flick. These are subjects reserved for those you know well.

To converse with someone you don't know, a comment about the weather is always a good opener that can lead to further conversation. If the person is wearing a sports hat or jacket, and you know something about that particular sport, then you've got a great conversation starter. Sports lovers love to talk about sports.

A sincere compliment is always a great way to strike up a conversation. You must be sincere because pretentiousness will be noticed. You don't want to alienate the person. Give them a chance to expand on the conversation by telling you something about whatever it was you complimented. This will lead to a more engaging conversation.

A psychological trick first described by Ben Franklin is to ask for a favor. For some reason, human nature perhaps, when someone does a favor for another person, it sparks a connection and makes the person more open to conversation. You don't need to ask a stranger anything elaborate. Something as simple as "Can you tell me how to get to room 200?" or "Can I borrow your pen for a moment?" is all you need to say. Most people will be happy to oblige.

Another great opener is to say something about the venue you're at. For example, if you're attending a conference and you see someone you'd like to converse with, you can point something out and make a comment about it. You could mention the seating arrangement or ask where the coffee is located, etc.

If you're in an office setting, you can mention a painting on the wall or construction taking place outside, or anything you see that can spark a discussion. Don't be shy. Most people will respond and be happy to engage in conversation with you.

Asking for someone's opinion is a form of flattery and is a sure way to begin conversing. You can start by saying, "Excuse me, I'm not from here. Could you recommend a good restaurant?" or "I see you have a Starbucks coffee. Do you know how their lattes are?"

All of these things, and more, can open the door to a conversation and a lasting relationship. Even if you never encounter the person again, you likely had an enjoyable exchange and one that made your day a little better.

## Ways to Make Your Conversation Interesting

*Ask something personal in connection with the topic*

You've made it through the conversation opener, now you need to keep the discussion moving. The next step is to keep things interesting. You can do this by bringing the conversation around to the other person. People love to talk about themselves, and you want to take the opportunity to do so.

You can segue into a more personal conversation by making the topic about them. For instance, if you're having a generic conversation about the weather, you could ask them if they've ever been to Florida or California, or lived through an earthquake or tornado. You could ask what climate they prefer, if they're sick of living in the cold and snow or if they loathe the heat and humidity.

If you're talking generically about the job market, you can ask what business they're in. There are literally hundreds of topics to discuss that you can gear toward the other person. And when they speak, give them your full attention.

Your goal is to learn more about those you meet, and that's why you'll want to bring the conversation to a more personal level, but not too personal. Asking a stranger if they're married and have children could easily send the person running. You don't want to come off as a creeper. Overly personal questions are out-of-bounds at this stage of the conversation.

Once you have the person talking about themselves, most often they will ask something about you. Don't overdo. This is where you want to contain your excitement that this person has an interest in learning something about you.

You don't want to ramble on about your spouse or kids or recent vacation, you want to be friendly, concise and answer what was asked of you. Don't use words that some might find offensive or inappropriate. For example, you don't want to tell someone you just met that you just got over a puking spell. This is a surefire way for the person to excuse themselves and head for the hills. And, yes, there are some who will speak that way to a stranger, and you don't want to be counted in that group.

Questions are always good to encourage engagement, and there are a plethora of things you can ask. Stay away from topics that are controversial, such as politics, vaccinations or any topic that can result in a heated debate.

When you attempt a conversation with someone you don't know or someone you've only interacted with briefly, if they aren't interested in talking with you, don't take it personally. Politely excuse yourself and leave.

You have to be aware that not everyone is friendly, or you may have encountered an introvert who isn't comfortable speaking with strangers. It is a normalcy that you're going to run into from time to time. Never force a conversation. If the person doesn't say anything, but their body language sends a message of discomfort, you need to leave the conversation as soon as possible, and politely do so.

*Bowing out in a group*

Say, you and your coworkers go out for a drink after work. You're all sitting at a table and the conversation turns to the boss. The others are speaking negatively, and you aren't comfortable bashing the boss. You know it could get back to them, and you aren't of the same opinion.

What do you do? You know that soon, one of your coworkers will turn to you and ask you to opine or ask if you agree with something.

This is where the social skill of knowing when to exit comes into play. You can do one of several things to escape. You can pretend you got a text message telling you that you need to leave to pick up one of your kids, or go to your mother's house for something... of course, it's not good to be dishonest but it's worse to have to partake in a conversation that makes you uncomfortable. Added to that, you disagree with what they're saying and that can lead to a debate if you state your feelings. Debates can quickly turn into arguments, especially if those you are with are drinking alcohol. So, it's best to find an excuse to leave.

Just remember your excuse should someone say something to you about it the next day. If a coworker asks if you were on time picking up your son from his baseball practice, you don't want to be caught off-guard and say, "Huh?" That's a sure sign that you fabricated your way out of the group.

# Chapter 4: The downside, How to Improve Your Listening Skills

Appropriate communication is very important in today's highly stressful, high-tech, and high-speed world. Genuine listening is becoming rare because people devote less time to listening to what the other person is saying. Therefore, there is a need to develop good listening skills that can help to build relationships, ensure understanding, resolve conflicts, solve problems, and enhance accuracy.

*The less you speak, the more you will hear."* - Alexander Solshenitsen

## Listen Actively

The outcome of effective listening in the workplace is that less time is wasted and there are fewer errors. The beneficial result of listening actively at home includes the development of self-reliant and resourceful children who have the ability to solve problems on their own. Listening builds careers and friendships. It saves marriages and money.

Here are some tips that can help you in developing good listening skills.

*Face the person who is speaking and keep eye contact*

Trying to talk to a person who is looking at various things in the room, studying what is given on the screen of a computer, or gazing through the window is like making an effort to hit a moving target. The person's attention is divided between so many things and you may get fifty percent or just five percent of it.

If you were talking to your child, you could ask him to look at you when you are talking. But you cannot order a friend, lover, or colleague to do that.

In the Western culture, eye contact is a basic component of good communication. When you speak, you should look at the other person and they should look at you.

However, this does not mean that a conversation cannot be carried on from different parts of the room. But when the conversation goes on for some time, the people who are speaking will move to the same place to communicate properly.

You should have the courtesy to put away your books, papers, phone, or any other distractions and turn toward the person who is speaking to you. Some people may not be able to maintain eye contact due to shyness, guilt, shame, uncertainty, or cultural taboos. You can excuse them and remain focused.

Look at people, and talk even if the others do not do the same with you.

*Be attentive and relaxed*

After making eye contact, you can relax. There is no need to stare at your partner continually. Look away from time to time when speaking. But you should pay full attention to what is being said.

According to the dictionary to "attend" to another person implies:

- Being present
- Giving attention
- Applying or directing yourself
- Paying attention
- Being ready to do service

Keep all distractions, such as noise and background activity away from your mind. Do not concentrate on the speech mannerisms or accent of the speaker and become distracted. Above all, do not allow your own feelings, biases, and thoughts distract you.

*Do not be judgmental*

Listen to the other individual without mentally criticizing or judging what they are saying. Do not jump to conclusions. The person who is speaking is expressing their feelings and thoughts through the medium of language. You cannot know their thoughts until you listen to what they are saying.

Do not grab sentences. For example, if you are unable to slow down your mental pace and listen effectively, you may be tempted to rush the speaker by interrupting as they are speaking and finishing their sentences. Such a conversation does not work because both individuals follow their own thoughts and do not know what the other person is actually thinking or trying to say.

*Create a picture in your mind*

Listen to what the person is saying and make a mental picture based on the information that is being conveyed. If you are focused and your senses are fully alert, your brain can arrange the abstract concepts and give you a clear picture of what is being communicated. If someone speaks for a long time, you can concentrate on the key phrases and words that are used.

During a conversation, when it is your chance to listen to what the other person is saying, do not use that time to plan what you will say next. It is not possible to rehearse what you are going to say and also listen to the other person. You can do only one thing at a time. So you should pay attention only to what the speaker is saying.

Above all, you should focus on what the speaker is saying, even if you are bored. In case your thoughts wander, instantly force your mind to refocus on the speaker's words.

*Do not interrupt or impose solutions*

It is considered rude if you interrupt when someone is speaking. If a person interrupts it can mean that he is trying to show:

- They are more important.
- They are going to say something that is more accurate, relevant, or interesting.
- They do not care for what the other person thinks.
- They do not have time to listen to the other person's opinion.
- It is not a conversation. It is actually a contest in which he is going to be the winner.

Everyone has a different pace of thinking and speaking. If you can think and talk quickly, it is your responsibility to slow down your pace to match that of the speaker who is slow and more thoughtful, or who has difficulty in expressing himself.

If someone talks to you about their problems, do not start suggesting solutions. Mostly people prefer to find their own solutions. What they actually want from you is to listen. However, if you have a fantastic solution for their problem you can ask them if they would like to know your ideas.

*Ask questions when there is a pause*

You can ask questions if you do not understand something. But do this when there is a pause instead of interrupting the speaker. You can say that you could not understand what the speaker said about a particular topic.

*Do not ask questions and distract the person from the topic*

Sometimes it happens that a person is talking about his trip and the exciting things he did there. During the conversation he happens to mention the name of a friend who you have not seen for a long time. Do not start asking too many questions about that friend and his family. This will divert the conversation from the trip that he was describing and make it focus on that mutual friend.

If your question leads the conversation astray, it is your responsibility to bring it back once again to the actual topic. So you can say that it was nice to talk about that friend, but at present you would like to hear more about the person's trip.

*Express empathy*

Empathy is very important for effective listening. You should feel the way the speaker feels. For example, if the speaker expresses sadness you also feel sad, you feel joyful when he expresses joy, or fearful when he describes his fears. You can convey these feelings through your words or facial expressions.

To experience the feelings of the speaker, you should imagine yourself to be in the speaker's place. This may not be easy, and you may have to concentrate and make a lot of effort to do this.

Chapter 5 go deep into empathy topic.

*Give regular feedback*

You can show the speaker that you can understand his feelings by saying things that reflect the feelings of the speaker. For example, you can say that the speaker would have been thrilled, or it may have been a great ordeal for the speaker.

If the feelings of the speaker are not clear, you can paraphrase what has been said. You can show through suitable facial expressions that you understand his feelings. In this way, the speaker will know you are paying attention to what is being said and not indulging in some fantasies of your own.

*Note the nonverbal cues*

We can get to know a lot of things about each other without saying anything. While talking on the phone, we can sense the mood of a person through the tone of their voice. When we talk to a person, we can observe their facial expressions and body language whether they are enthusiastic, bored, or irritated. Therefore, you should not ignore these cues while listening.

## The Five-Step Method for an effective Listening

The five-step method can help you to acquire the skill of effective listening. For this, you should use a resource that has both audio as well as a written script. First, you should listen to the audio without referring to the text. After that you can use the transcript to check whether you have understood the audio correctly.

You can choose any of the following tools for practice:

- A clip from a TV show or movie along with the subtitles
- An audio book with a printed version
- A podcast with a transcript
- A video from any news site plus a transcript

- A video from YouTube with the available transcription or subtitles

It is ideal to start with one short clip of three to four minutes instead of using a long one. The reasons for doing this are:

- Long clips may be suitable for those who have reached a certain level of advancement, but they can be exhausting for a beginner.

- Repetition occupies an important place in the learning procedure. If the clips are short, it is easier to hear the audio again and again.

- Listening to short clips and learning them well has more value than using longer ones and not gaining in depth knowledge.

Another thing that you should keep in mind while choosing your material is that it should be related to topics that are important to you.

*Listen to audio without reading*

Listen to audio without reading the text beforehand. Do not refer to it while listening. Focus only on the aural skills. See how far you are able to comprehend without the help of a visual aid.

In the beginning, this exercise may be a little difficult for you, so do not try to understand each and every word that is said, and instead focus on comprehending the gist or the main points of what is spoken.

Note some of the key phrases or words that can help you to understand what is being said.

*Repeat*

Do not be in a hurry to look at the transcript. Your purpose is to enhance your skills of listening, so continue to focus on listening.

Play the clip once again and listen carefully. There may be some key phrases or words that you may not have noted earlier, make a note of them. Now that you are a little familiar with the context of the piece you may be able to comprehend better.

You should listen to the piece three to four times. You will be able to improve your comprehension bit by bit each time and grasp each word correctly.

*Read*

After that, you can see the written text. Read it and see whether what you understood through listening is correct. Is the gist that you comprehended correct?

Note whether there are new words and words that sound different when they are spoken. See if you understood them correctly. If you did not follow any of those words, listen to them carefully when you play the audio again.

*Use both audio and text*

After reading the text and checking the words that you did not comprehend you will have a better understanding of what has been said. The next step is to listen to the piece and refer to the text while listening. You can do this two to three times.

During this stage you will use both aural as well as visual stimuli. You should make the best use of this facility and connect the spoken words to the written words.

*Listen to the audio once again*

Finally, you should only listen to the audio two to three times without referring to the transcript. By then you may be in a position to grasp everything that is being said without any visual assistance from a text.

# Chapter 5: They love you because you are empathetic

Empathy refers to the ability of a person to see things through the other person's perspective.

Dale Carnegie said, "If there's one secret of success it lies in the ability to get the other's point of view and see things from that person's angle as well as your own."

A person who is highly empathetic can sense the feelings of the people around him and possesses the capacity to tap into the same feelings within himself. In other words, he is able to truly experience the emotions of the person he is empathizing with.

There is a difference between empathy and sympathy. When a person is sympathetic he pities the other individual and there is some distance between them. But when a person is empathetic, he knows and understands the other person's feelings and also feels the same. So a sympathetic person feels sorry for the other person while an empathetic person feels what the other person is feeling.

Empathy is beneficial for everyone. When a person expresses empathy, he builds a genuine human connection. The person who receives empathy feels that he is understood, valued, and respected. The empathizer establishes himself as a memorable, trustworthy, and likeable person.

*"The most basic of all human needs is the need to understand and be understood."* - Ralph Nichols

## Best Ways to Express Empathy

*Listen*

Listening to people is a very effective way of demonstrating empathy. You engage yourself in active listening, which means you listen with a purpose. You paraphrase whatever the person has said and express your emotions. Your emotional reactions form an important component of empathy. They enable the person to regulate his own emotions and responses.

*Open up*

It is not enough if you just listen to someone, you have to open up emotionally to the person. Only then can you build a deeper connection with them.

Empathy involves sharing vulnerabilities. To practice empathy in the true sense, a person has to share his inner space with someone who reciprocates his feelings.

However, you need not share your life with each and every person you come across. You can choose the person you want to open up to. After identifying the person, you should try to show your feelings regarding a particular topic instead of leaning on opinions in a conversation. Speak in "first person" or use 'I' to start the sentences. For instance, "I am happy we got a chance to spend some time together."

You should never answer a question by saying that you do not know. Make an effort to think of an answer that expresses your feelings. If you absolutely can't think of an answer, you can ask the person you're conversing with to elaborate so that you can provide a better answer. Whatever you do, don't try to "fake it until you make it." The other person will see right through that. You want to do your best to comprehend the question and ask questions if you don't understand.

*Show physical affection*

It is not possible to do this with everyone. So you should first ask the person if it is all right. The expression of physical affection can enhance the levels of oxytocin. It can make both the individuals feel better.

If you are quite familiar with the person, you can give them a hug, put your arm around their shoulder, or place your hand on their arm. This will show that you are focusing your attention on them and also create a loving connection between both of you.

Oxytocin helps people to interpret the emotions of others in a better way. So a hug may build up both their and your emotional intelligence.

Don't hesitate to ask, "May I give you a hug," or say, "I can take your hand and walk with you."

You never want to place your hands on anyone without knowing that it's okay to do so. If you aren't sure, ask. Don't assume anything. In today's personal space climate, your good intentions can be misinterpreted, and that's the last thing you need.

*Notice everything that is going on around you*

Focus on your surroundings. Observe the actions, expressions, and feelings of everyone around you. Think about the feelings of the people with whom you interact.

Observe and register the sights, sounds, and smells consciously. Studies have shown that when you practice mindfulness about the people who are near you and your surroundings, there is a greater likelihood of extending empathy toward them and helping someone when he needs it.

*Avoid judging others*

Judgment, we've already brought that up since is a very important factor when you are practicing mindfulness and empathy.

Generally, people have a tendency to judge others when they meet or interact with them for the first time. But this has to be avoided if you want to be empathetic.

It does not matter whether the person is wrong or right. You have to try to understand his perspective more deeply. This will enable you to develop empathy toward him.

However, this does not mean that you should accept wrong behavior.

Human nature has us making wrong judgments from time to time. Have you ever met someone and thought right off the bat that you didn't like them? That they were pompous? Have you mistaken shyness for arrogance? We can misjudge others. Often, we can get to know a person better and realize our initial thoughts were completely off-base. This is why you want to avoid passing judgment on someone you just met or don't know well.

We also don't know what the other person might be going through in their personal life. That's why we need to stop judging before we get to know a person.

*Offer to help the other person*

When you offer help, it is a sign that you are aware of the person's suffering and wish to make their life easier. It is a remarkable expression of empathy. You are ready to spend your precious time on doing something for a person without asking for anything in return.

There are plenty of ways you can help people. You can offer help in simple ways, such as keeping the door open for the next person who is entering a building or buying coffee for someone who is behind you. Also, you can help an elderly person by setting up a computer for them, or you can look after someone's children when they want to go out for some urgent work.

Even if you just offer to help someone, it is an empathetic act. For example, you can open the way for your friend to get support and help from you by saying that if they need anything, they can ask you.

## The Responses to be Avoided

There are some responses that should be avoided if you wish to be empathetic when a person shares something about his difficult situation with you.

*Do not dodge*

When someone tells you about their unhappy situation, do not try to shift the conversation to another topic or start checking your phone. Do not try to give an excuse and leave the place in a rush.

The other individual may feel lost and terribly lonely. They might be afraid to open up with anyone in the future.

*Look for the silver lining*

Some people feel uncomfortable when someone talks about their problems, so they tell that person to look at the brighter side of things. They say that everything happens for a reason.

This sort of response is all right in theory. However, it does not help the person in any way. When a person is in pain, they do not wish to hear all this.

*Try to minimize things*

When a person talks about their problems, some people try to talk about it in a light manner. They try to make their problems appear smaller so that they may somehow end the conversation. Otherwise, they just keep silent about it and try to convey that the other person is not going through a bad situation. They do not make any attempt to understand or connect with the person's feelings.

*Give advice*

Usually, when people face medical difficulties, their friends and relatives start offering a number of solutions for their problems. They suggest various therapies and treatments. But they fail to provide the person with what is most needed during such a challenging time. They need someone to listen and be by their side.

*Tell stories*

Sometimes people feel uncomfortable when a person talks about their struggles, so they start telling a story of a person who faced a similar situation. This may be a harmless gesture, but many times the story that they tell is not very similar and ends badly. So it does not turn out to be helpful or encouraging.

You probably have heard of the pregnant lady who doesn't want to hear another labor story, or how much heartburn they had in the last few months before delivery, or how they know someone who knows the cousin of someone who had gestational diabetes.

Remember, misery doesn't want company, especially when a person is suffering.

*Talk about a worse case*

As above, there is no use trying to console someone by telling them that there is someone who is going through a worse situation. A person who is suffering cannot gain anything by knowing that their pain is lesser than another. This is such a critical fact to remember. In as much as we think it helps, it doesn't.

*Overreact*

Do not create a scene and respond in a dramatic manner when someone talks about their woes.

You can sympathize, but don't showcase their troubles. Keep a level head and calm voice at all times.

# Tips to Develop Empathy

*Take interest in people*

Be interested in knowing about people who aren't in your circle of friends. For example, the people who travel on the public bus with you or those you meet when you are standing in line at a coffee shop.

You should be interested in understanding the other person's world a little. For this, you may have to tell them about yourself and be open.

If someone looks at you, give them a smile. See if there is something in the surroundings that can be used as a pretext to start the conversation. For example, if the person has a book in their hand, you can make a comment about it, or ask the person to help or explain something. You can smile and continue the conversation. If you know the name of the person, you can use it sporadically during the conversation.

However, there are some people who might not like to talk or interact with strangers. For example, they may continue to read a book when you approach them, they may wear headphones, face away from people, or not make eye contact. You should understand their behavior and leave them alone. This is also a part of empathy.

Another thing that you should keep in mind is that you should take due care of yourself while interacting with strangers. Listen to your instincts. If you feel uncomfortable or threatened while talking to a person, stop the interaction and leave.

*Work as a volunteer*

If you wish to become empathetic toward others you should work as a volunteer. Volunteering can help you to understand people's needs and connect with new people. Dedicating some time to the needy people is also beneficial for a person's mental health.

You can research and find out the organizations where they need volunteers. For example, you can work at any homeless shelter or for an organization like Red Cross.

*Overcome your prejudices*

Many times it happens that you get stuck with your prejudices. Your notions may not always be right, so you should analyze them. Learn to see each individual in the correct light. Look for something that is similar between you and the other person. Use that similarity to connect with them.

Get rid of your biases, such as those who have mental health problems are dangerous or all those who are poor are lazy or

Many of these are based on the wrong information. So acquire proper knowledge about these things.

*Imagination*

Imagination is very useful for developing empathy toward others. You may not experience everything that the other person goes through; however, you can imagine and get an idea of his feelings. Actively imagining the suffering of another person can enable you to empathize with him.

So when you see an old man begging on the roadside, you should not think that he may spend the money that he is given on alcohol or cigarettes. Instead, you can imagine how they must be feeling because they have to spend their life on the roadside and no one shows any mercy.

It has been found that those who read a lot of fiction are able to understand emotions, intentions, and behaviors in a better way. So it may be helpful to read extensively and develop your imagination.

*Experiential empathy*

Try to experience someone's life directly by living like them for some time. For example, you can perform all the tasks of your mother for one week. In this way, you can discover the hardships that she has to face in managing the house as well as go out for work. This will enable you to appreciate the amount of work she does and you may decide to help her with the chores.

*Give importance to each one*

Do not consider yourself to be superior. Each individual has their own importance in the world. Every person has some strengths and some flaws. You should not put them into typical groups and label them.

*Meditation*

Meditation is not only helpful for dealing with anxiety and stress, it is also useful for developing empathy. You can sit in a quiet place and watch your breath. Visualize that you are worthy of receiving loving kindness. Do not think about your flaws or your strengths.

After getting loving kindness for yourself, practice it for four different kinds of people.

- A person you respect such as a teacher/boss
- A dear one such as a friend or family member
- A neutral individual such as someone at the shop or a person you have seen outside on that day

- A hostile individual such as someone you have disagreed with

To remain on the right track, you can repeat "loving kindness" like a mantra. This will remind you and help you to concentrate on having loving kindness toward all of them, even the hostile individual.

*Practicing Empathy in the Workplace*

Often, people think that empathy is meant only for their personal lives. According to them, empathy is to be expressed while comforting their daughter who has had a breakup, listening to the woes of a frustrated spouse, pacifying a friend who is mourning, and other such situations.

However, empathy should also be expressed in professional relationships. For example, when you work in a business that is based on referrals and relationships the connections are formed because there is a basic trust between your network and you.

If you show empathy toward people you make them feel that you do not just listen to them but you hear them, and they are understood because they are heard. This makes the people in your network feel connected and safe, so they are able to trust you and your business.

## Express vulnerability

Mostly, professional conversations remain within emotionally "safe zones." They stay away from expressing vulnerability.

However, a person should not hesitate to ask someone for help in the workplace. If you ask someone for help you show vulnerability. This vulnerability can often lead to a better connection between you and the other person.

Three steps for showing more vulnerability in professional interactions are:

- After listening carefully to what a person has to say, think about a time when you went through a similar experience. For instance, a project on which you were working might have failed because the team members did not get along with each other.

- Try to recollect the feelings that you experienced at that time. Maybe you were anxious and disappointed.

- Convey those feelings and emotions to them. Then share the things that you learned from the experience.

When you share your own mistakes and insecurities with others, you can connect with them in a much better way.

*Do not use assumptions*

Assumptions are not suitable when you want to be empathetic. Having assumptions implies that you have preconceived ideas that are formed without experience or true understanding.

As we've already discussed, assumptions are not a good thing. We will look into a couple more reasons why.

Sometimes people try to assume things and take a shortcut to solve problems. But when you take shortcuts, you do not see the complete picture. Consequently, you do not really 'solve' the issue. When you try to solve a problem on the basis of an assumption you may not understand a person's problem correctly. Therefore, the connection that you are trying to make will feel as if it is unnatural and forced.

The person whose problem you are trying to solve may think that you do not understand their problem, and they should not seek your help in future as you do not listen properly. They might withdraw.

You should not try to empathize until you understand the scenario correctly. Spend a little extra time to listen properly and ask questions. Only after that you should try to connect and empathize with others.

# Chapter 6: Outside of work. How to Meet People and Make New Friends

If you have good friends, your life can be much more enjoyable. You can have fun with them on weekends, go on adventures and trips with them and learn something new from them. You can also share the experiences and stories of your life with them.

In the absence of friends, you may have to live a dull and lonely life. So it is essential to meet people and make friends.

If you want to meet new people you should put yourself in certain social settings where there is more scope for meeting interesting people. You should be in such surroundings where it is easy to socialize. The people you meet will surely bring some joy to you even though all of them may not become your friends ultimately.

## Opportunities for Meeting New People

*Take part in sports*

You can join a sports club and take part in various sports and other activities. You may go for hiking or biking with a group of people or become a member of a softball or tennis team.

Look for a group that is involved in a physical activity that you enjoy. Engage the members in a conversation and suggest that you meet for coffee, beer, or wine after the activity or game.

When you go for a hike you can spot the individuals who are sociable and almost the same age as you and start a conversation. It is easy to make friends in beautiful natural surroundings where there are no distractions from day to day life. Moreover, you can share your passion for outdoor sports.

*Book clubs*

If you are fond of reading, you can join a book club. It will give you a wonderful opportunity to connect with new people who have similar interests like you. If you are interested in joining one you can inquire at the local bookstore or search online. You can join different clubs and see where you can find a group of people who enjoy reading the same books like you and are fond of socializing.

If you do not find the right club that suits your tastes, start a club of your own. Invite people to join it.

*Writing groups*

If you like to write or have been thinking about it, most communities have writing groups. They are a great way to make new friends and get feedback on your work. If you have a novel inside of you that you haven't started, you will certainly get the encouragement you need from the members of a writing group.

You will enjoy being with like-minded people who are genuine in their wishes for your success. Those in writing groups tend to be very compassionate people, and when you are comfortable being in the group, you can begin to share personal tidbits. Writers are creative people, and not only are they willing to help, they are willing to listen.

*Meetup*

You can visit MeetUp.com and find various group activities that you might be interested in. Go through the events that are taking place in your area and take part in one or more. For example, you can find networking groups, social groups, and book clubs through Meetup.

*Talk to your neighbors*

Sometimes we have very nice people who live near us, but we never speak to them and miss the chance of making some good friends. Reach out to them. You may find that they have all the qualities that you are looking for in a friend.

When you see someone who is working in their yard you can offer to help. You can start a conversation about something going on in your neighborhood or community. You can find something in common to talk about, and open the gate from there.

Around the holidays, you can bake cookies or brownies for your neighbors. They will appreciate the kindness.

If you have someone new move in to you neighborhood, bring them a houseplant, or if weather permits, bring them an outdoor plant. It will make them feel welcome, and they will surely thank you.

*Converse with people around you*

Wherever you go, whether it is a grocery store, concert or post office, start talking to someone there. You should keep some conversation starters ready with you so that you can break the ice and start talking.

There was once a man at my post office during the holiday rush when line were long, who started doing magic tricks. He entertained everyone in the line and some people took his name and contact information. He utilized his social skills to not only entertain but to make friends. These situations can result in lasting friendships.

You can also be in line at a grocery store and try to small talk the person behind you, who will simply look away from you.

These are the people you want to avoid. As stated earlier, don't force yourself on anyone. Turn around and say no more.

Have you ever been in a store and small-talked a cashier who just gives you a blank stare? Those are the most uncomfortable situations, but they do happen and there's nothing you can do except to apologize. You can say, "I'm sorry to have interrupted you. Have a good day."

*Use community tables*

Look for restaurants that provide the facility for sitting at bar tables or dinner tables. Do not sit in an isolated manner on tables that accommodate just two persons. Sitting at community tables offers a wonderful chance to strike a conversation with strangers seated nearby.

If you stay at a bed and breakfast inn, this is a great way to meet others as the meals are often served with all guests present at the table. You might also share other facilities, such as porch swings and chairs, or boating, etc.

*Reach out to people through social media*

Visit various social media sites and look for people who live in your area. Reach out to them and ask them out for coffee.

You might discover your old acquaintances or friends who have moved to some place nearby when you go through Facebook. You can reconnect with them.

You can also check the profiles of various people on the social sites and look for those who have something in common with you. Try to contact them and see if they reciprocate properly. You can continue the interaction until you build a good friendship.

You want to be careful, and always meet in a public place. You don't need to put yourself in danger. And never give too much personal information if the person is unknown to you. Be sure if you're going to meet with a stranger that you met online that you let someone know where you will be and the time you will be there. Better yet, have a friend nearby. For instance, if you meet at a coffee shop, have a friend sitting in the shop when you arrive. You need to pretend you don't know them.

And as many of us have done in the past when we are with someone we might not want to be with, have a friend call or text with a reason to leave. That works every time!

*Host a party*

You can host a casual party and invite people who live in your neighborhood, work in the same place as you, or acquaintances. Tell them that they can bring their friends along with them.

This will increase the scope of meeting new people or potential friends.

You need not have an elaborate party. Even some soup and pizzas are sufficient. The aim is to make people come together and to expand your social circle.

*Go for a walk with your dog*

If you have a dog, when you go walking, surely, there will be people who will stop to admire it and ask you questions about breed, gender, etc. It will give people an excuse to start a conversation with you. Moreover, there may be other people who are taking their pets out for a walk. Your pet may attract the attention of those pets who may drag their masters to you. This may give you a chance to meet new people.

If you are lucky to have a park for dogs in the area, you can take a frisbee or ball with you when you take your pet there for an outing. This may give you a chance to mingle and make friends with other dog lovers over there.

*Business associations*

Connect with associations or groups that are associated with your career. You can research and find out the business events that are going on in your area. Attend them and connect with the other participants professionally as well as personally.

Most professions have organizations. Lawyers have bar associations, the media has press clubs, teachers have associations as do business owners. Don't be shy. Join and volunteer.

*Go to the gym*

A gym is a very suitable place for meeting new people. When you attend a gym class, you get a chance to meet many new people who are interested in doing physical exercise, losing weight, or are health conscious just like you.

If there is a juice bar or cafe at the gym, you can hang out with the others after completing your workout.

The same goes for exercise classes. Whether it's Zumba or Crossfit or Parkour or even a snowshoeing class or canoeing class, you're bound to meet many new people.

*Ask someone to introduce you to friends*

If some of your friends have a wide social circle you can ask them for introductions. For example, if you move to another place you may not know many people. At such times, you can ask your close friend who already knows a lot of people there to make an introduction. They can send an email to their friends and introduce you. Then you can follow up and meet them for coffee or dinner.

*Join a speaking club*

Mostly, public speaking is not everyone's cup of tea. But when you join a speaking club you are with a group of people who have the same learning curve and similar fears. This gives them a common ground to interact more freely with each other.

Speaking clubs help a person to become more confident about making presentations and also give him an opportunity to meet various interesting people.

Toastmasters is one such organization for public speaking, and you will meet many people will a common interest.

*Attend cultural events*

You can become a member of the local theater, symphony, or ballet group. Attend the fundraising events and the performances. Start conversations with other people who come to attend the function. They come because they also appreciate art like you. So you may find something common to strike a friendship.

If you are fond of visual art you can visit the local galleries or exhibitions and discuss art with the organizers or guests.

*Brew tours*

If you live in some place where there a number of breweries you can join a brew tour. Many wineries and restaurants offer wine tasting facility. By participating in a beer or wine tour you can meet connoisseurs and also have fun. Beer and wine always pair well with socializing.

*Attend seminars*

Take a look at the local community calendar and find the events that are going to take place in the area. Attend the seminars and other functions. While doing so try to find a seat next to a person who may also be on the lookout for a friend like you.

*Go to a music club*

If you are a lover of music and like jazz or any other genre that is suitable for having a conversation in a small place you can join a low key music club. You can have a great conversation with new people and also enjoy great music.

*Dance classes*

Ballroom dancing gives an opportunity to get close to new friends and have personal contact with romantic partners. However, it is not necessary to stick to ballroom dance alone. You can join a class for learning Salsa dancing or Zumba. It is great for exercising as well as for meeting people who love to have fun.

*Visit a museum*

Usually there are several museums in cities that cater to the interests of different people. For those who are fond of art, science or natural history, a museum can be a very suitable place for meeting new people. You can talk to other people who come to visit the museum and chat about the things that you have seen.

*Art classes*

When you join any class, you automatically come into contact with many people who have similar interests. You can enroll in an art class where you have to do things together instead of listening to a lecture. This will give you a chance to converse with the other students. You should introduce yourself and initiate a conversation with them.

Whether it's watercolor or pottery classes, you can interact with the participants. It's a great way to meet others and to get feedback on your work and give others feedback.

*Join a nonprofit organization*

Those who like to support a cause that is particularly meaningful for them can become a member of a charitable association. As a decision-maker or leader in such an organization they can meet a wide variety of people who extend their support for the same cause.

*Coffee house*

If you work from home you may have to stay in your house most of the time. That means you may not be able to meet any new people or make friends. So you should take your computer to a local coffee house and do your work there. You can continue your work and also look up once in a while to survey the people who come and go. It is also possible to talk to the person who is sitting on the table beside you. This person could become a good friend.

*Go to a bar*

You may find it intimidating to dine alone at a restaurant. You can go to the bar and have a conversation with the bartender as well as the other people who are there. Remember, don't sit and look at your phone or read a book. Instead, be friendly and approachable.

*Make the best use of invitations*

Do not turn down any invitations that you may get for social events. They offer a great opportunity to meet people. Even if the event is about something in which you are not at all interested do not miss it. If you do not like it you can leave whenever you like.

*Visit a farmers' market*

If you are fond of eating healthy food and enjoy cooking, farmers' markets can be fun for you. There you will find lots of people who have similar food values like you.

It will give you a chance to speak to the farmers, ask them questions, and also have a conversation with the other shoppers. There is a festive and sociable atmosphere at such events. You should take advantage of them and meet new people.

*Don't skip your class reunion*

Class reunions are a great way to rekindle old friendships and make new ones. If you went to a large school, chances are you never got to know all of your classmates. It's a perfect way to reacquaint yourself with classmates.

Chances are you won't run out of things to talk about, as reminiscing about school days is a subject most people enjoy, especially at reunions. Talking about the past and learning what your classmates are doing and hearing about their families and jobs is fun, and it can reestablish connections that were lost with time.

The more years that pass, the more classmates will generally show up for reunions. Make it a point to attend them all. If you were shy in school, and are not longer that same person, you can show how you've evolved over the years.

## Smart Ways of Making Friends

There are six important steps to meet people and make friends quickly. They are:

- Identify your favorite subject, hobby, or sport.
- Find the meetup groups or forums associated with that subject.
- Pick out the interest groups which meet regularly for discussing the subject.
- Participate in their meetings.

- Speak about things such as when was it that you started liking the subject or hobby, and how frequently you engage yourself in it.
- Jump to another conversation topic that is not connected with the key subject.

## Basic requirement for starting a friendship quickly

Sometimes people follow all the steps mentioned above, but even then they are not able to make new friends. The main reason for this is, it is not enough to have just one thing in common with the other person, two commonalities are needed for creating a friendship.

Whenever you take part in a social gathering and meet new people try to find the other common things between you besides the key subject for which the meeting is taking place.

The formula is as follows:

Potential friendship = 1st commonality + 2nd commonality

## Tips for Making Friends

If you wish to socialize you have to take the initiative. You cannot wait for someone to approach you. It is not that such things never happen. They do occur but they are rare. You have to make an effort to find friends.

Do not waste the weekend on frivolous tasks and hope that someone will text you. Instead of this, you should contact different people and find out their plans. See if it is feasible to join them. Otherwise, you can make a plan and ask others to join you. Do not hesitate to ask for company and think that it may look as if you are needy or desperate. In fact, it shows that you are a social person.

If others seem to be indifferent toward you, don't feel hurt. Many times people are too preoccupied and forget to include you in their social activities. It does not imply that they would not like to have you around them. Maybe you need to show more interest in their social activities to gain their attention.

Similarly, there may be some people who are slow in replying to emails or calling back. If you do not get an answer or if you get a delayed answer do not assume that they are trying to ignore or reject you. There is that word again—assume. It can't be stressed enough how bad assumptions are.

Do not be under the impression that it is very difficult to make friends. It is not as complex as you imagine it to be. Get rid of the inhibitions that you have about friendship.

You just need to meet someone you can get along and spend quality time with. It is not necessary to know each other for a very long time before becoming friends. Even if your relationship is not very deep or intimate, you can have a nice time and enjoy each other's company.

Do not be choosy if you are building your social circle from scratch. If you feel lonely, your first goal is to find someone who can give you company. So if you come across someone who is nice but not hundred percent ideal for being a friend, you can try to make friends with them. However, you should stay away from people who are toxic.

Socializing with people who are not as perfect as you want your friends to be is much better than staying alone and moping. Besides this, until you mix with different people you may not know much about people and their ways of interacting. Moreover, if you have a few friends it becomes easier to make more friends and expanding your social circle.

People who are lonely usually have a negative view of others. Those who are not the outgoing type are more choosy about the people they spend time with. So if you happen to be that kind of a person, try to overcome this attitude. Above all, you should not have a skewed image of yourself. Be realistic and understand your needs and circumstances correctly.

Another reason why a person may not like to hang around with someone is that they might have a very poor image of themselves and the other person seems to mirror their shortcomings. This is justified if they have some pesky traits and want to avoid those who have similar traits. However, there is a possibility of turning away some good individuals who happen to possess a few characteristics that tweak that person's insecurities slightly.

Don't get discouraged easily, and be persistent. When you join a club or your friend introduces you to his friends you may look forward to mixing with some wonderful people. But after you go there or mix with them, you have a disappointing experience. You start feeling that you lack the skills necessary for making friends. You may think that they are ignoring you or making fun of you.

But you should not give up so easily. Try mixing with these groups again. Often, the initial meeting may not be sufficient to connect with others properly.

If an individual does not accept your invitation as he is busy, do not get disheartened. Try again some other time. Do not jump to conclusions and assume that they don't like you or that no one likes you.

By giving an invitation, you have conveyed to the other person that you are fond of them. They might not be able to meet you this time, but they will start seeing you as a person they can have an enjoyable time with on some other occasion.

Be realistic while meeting a potential friend. Think about the place you occupy in their life and how much time it will take to become good friends. Be patient and wait for the right opportunity. If you are in a situation that is suitable for finding and making friends such as a college, team or club, it may not take much time to make friends.

In other situations, you may have to spend some time looking for like-minded people. After that, you may have to meet for some months to know each other properly. It may take a year to become really good friends.

If you have enough patience you can progress from the stage when you have no plans at all to the stage of having plans for every weekend with one person, to the next stage of having plans for two days every week with a number of people.

**Top Friend Making Hacks for Shy People**

Sometimes people who are shy wonder how they can make friends. It's a lot harder for those who are more reserved and feel awkward around others. It's not impossible to make friends, but it is more difficult.

For those who are shy, it's important that they socialize within their limits. This means not stepping out more than they are ready to do. It can take practice and self-confidence to meet others and feel relaxed.

For those who are timid, it can help to be in a group setting. That way, you won't have the awkwardness of a one-on-one conversation if things start going south.

When in a group, there's always someone to save you. Group settings can help you to become comfortable being around others, it can help you to overcome your shyness, and it can be a confidence-builder.

When you're in a social setting with a group of people, look approachable. That means to stand or sit in a position so that your body language tells others you're willing to have a conversation. You don't want to be a wallflower or sit with your hand covering a part of your face. You'll want to show some confidence, even if you aren't feeling it.

You should stand or sit so that you are visible to others. Someone might approach you who will do the following:

- Guide the conversation in such a way that you can open up.
- Attempt to make you feel comfortable.
- Invite you to meet their friends.

- Make you feel a part of whatever it is that's going on.

*Approaching a shy person*

When we see a shy person, we might want to approach them, especially if they look uncomfortable in a social setting.

Before you approach someone, you might want to ask around, in a stealth way, who the person is. They are there for a reason, and someone invited them, so you can learn something about that person before approaching them.

Say, for example, a friend tells you that they work with the shy person and they are an amazing artist. You now have a segue for your approach, especially if you know something about art.

Getting to know something about the person you want to approach makes for a more comfortable encounter.

You'll be able to read the person to know if they are interested in conversing or if you need to bow out gracefully.

This is something that can't be stressed enough. There are people who just don't want to be approached. They are content to be in their own world. They are enjoying themselves even if they don't appear to be.

There's nothing wrong with being a loner. It can't hold you back from certain things in life, but if that's your level of comfort, then don't feel guilty about it. As long as a person doesn't feel isolated and sink into a depression, keeping oneself company is not atypical.

We hear all the time about men who have "man caves," where they go for their alone time, away from family and life. We have all heard about women who lock themselves in their sewing rooms and get lost for hours in their projects. Everyone needs alone time, and there's nothing wrong with it.

When alone time turns to constants isolation, that's when it's best to seek professional help.

Whether you're shy or you want to approach someone who appears to be shy, remember our tips.

Friendships can be made and had with shy people. And you might be surprised how they will open up once they get to know you. Again, it can't be stressed enough—don't mistake shyness for arrogance. Timid people can send the wrong vibes, and you could miss out on an opportunity to make a great friend.

# Conclusion

People use various kinds of communication every day that includes verbal, nonverbal, visual, and written methods. Verbal communication involves speaking, while the nonverbal form is about communicating through eye contact, gestures, and facial expressions.

Nonverbal communication is referred to as body language. It is a significant tool that can determine a person's success in career as well as relationships. Nearly ninety-three percent of communication may take place through nonverbal cues. If you pay attention to your body language and the messages that are conveyed by it, you can improve your chances of being successful.

Social skills refer to the skills that facilitate communication. They have a lot of significance for everyone, irrespective of their position or level of experience. They help to make, maintain and develop relationships with your clients, new contacts, and colleagues.

Penelope Trunk said, "Getting or giving anything is about social skills. The world is about being comfortable where you are and making people comfortable, and that's what social skills are."

This book has provided you with much helpful advice to up your game when it comes to socialization. Whether you're an introvert or extrovert, there is something in this book for everyone.

It's important to remember that social skills are learned when we are children, and we learn them from the adults and social situations around us. Sometimes, we want to be the opposite of our parents or the person who raised us, and that's okay.

For example, a child who is raised by a loud, boisterous father might be more passive as an adult. Perhaps their father had embarrassed them in front of their peers once, or many times, and they don't want to be the same way.

Social skills are learned, and they are learned at any age. You can find social skills groups in many communities. These groups will help those who are shy, socially awkward, or anxious in social settings.

Before we leave you, it's important to mention a few words about social anxiety. This can cause panic attacks if not properly managed.

Visualize this scenario: You are at an office party that you were mandated to attend. You didn't want to go, and you had anxiety about it even before you stepped foot in the venue. You don't know why you feel the way you do because the only attendees will be coworkers, yet you are dreading it.

You dress for the occasion, take a deep breath, and make up your mind to enjoy yourself. You arrive and look around. The room is dark with only ceiling lights shining down on the crowd. And there is a crowd. You scan the room, looking for all of the exit doors. You want to make certain you can exit quickly in the event of a fire or other emergency.

Your boss sees you and approaches. He takes you by the arm and walks you to the bar where he buys you a drink. You really want alcohol to relax you , but you opt for a soda. He tells you to meander and talk to everyone. You nod and slowly walk away, feeling as if you can't breathe. Your throat feels as if it's constricting, and you need air. You're in the middle of the room and you have to push through huddles of people to get near the door. Your heart is racing, you can feel your pulse pounding in your neck, and lightheadedness takes over.

Finally, you get to the door and walk outside. You find your car and sit inside, debating on whether to leave. You decide home is the safest place at the moment, so you head home without saying goodbye to anyone.

If this situation sounds like something you've experienced, you don't want to let it go untreated. Social anxiety can eventually jeopardize your job and your relationships. Social anxiety can lead to avoidant personality disorder.

This needed to be mentioned so that if you recognize yourself in the above scenario, you will seek help or find a social anxiety support group.

## Ways to enhance social skills

If you are earnest to bring about an improvement in your social interactions, you can do the following:

**Get honest feedback:** You can ask your mentors, managers, or close friends to give you honest feedback regarding your social skills and let you know the areas in which you need to improve. You can ask about your personality, and ask them to point out your flaws. Don't take offense. Remember, they are helping and you did ask them to be honest.

**Set goals:** You can set measurable goals for acquiring a set of good social skills on the basis of the insights that they offer.

**Practice:** After you know the tips and tactics for improving social skills start practicing them at work and at home. You can even work as a volunteer or take part in some activity where you can put the interpersonal skills into practice without much pressure.

**Rid yourself of negative thoughts:** Negativity can bring us down and those around us. One person in a bad mood can impact others. Teachers see this in classrooms all the time. One negative student can set the mood for the others, and it will carry on throughout the day.

Instead of thinking of yourself as sitting in a corner at a party with no one to speak with, think of yourself as a great conversationalist who others will want to engage with. Positive thoughts will yield positive results.

You will find the more positive your attitude, the more people will want to be around you. The more negative you are, the less likely you'll draw a crowd or even one person. No one wants to be around negativity. As we said at the beginning of this book, people don't want to be around Debbie and Donnie Downer.

We hope this book has helped you to improve your social skills, and we wish you feel more comfortable in your daily relationships. Always remember, you are the architect of your social relationships and the master of your emotions, you lead!